Mastering Multiple Choice

The Definitive Guide to Better Grades
on Multiple Choice Exams

Stephen Merritt

brainranch
personal & business development publishing

Published in Canada by The Brain Ranch
info@thebrainranch.com

ISBN 0-9739782-1-X

CONTENTS

INTRODUCTION

INTRODUCTION

THE LAST FEW DECADES have shown an massive increase in the use of multiple choice as the primary method of measuring student success. Increasingly, students are discovering that their final grade is determined by as few as one or two multiple choice exams.

In fact, in many programs, your academic success is being determined *entirely* by multiple choice exams. Period. Regardless of your topic of study, if you haven't mastered the art of taking multiple choice exams, you're at risk of doing more poorly than you should.

As of this writing, it's been estimated that **students in North America complete a staggering *half a billion* multiple choice tests per year**. What's even more staggering is how many students will do more poorly than they should – or crash and burn altogether – because they lack proper test-taking skills.

Tests like the SAT, MCAT, or LSAT, which allow entrance to graduate and post-graduate schooling are almost entirely multiple choice. From exam halls to distance education, from weekend certificate courses to doctorate degrees, multiple choice exams are determining the course of your future.

> **If you're in any kind of educational environment, multiple choice exams are determining the course of your future.**

Sound scary? It should.

What can you do about it? Well, you could protest at your school, write your government representatives, and stage exam boycotts on campus.

Or you can, like many other smart students, learn to *use these tests to your advantage*. Yes, that's right. From here on, multiple choice tests are your best friend come exam time.

Research shows that students can perform significantly better on objective tests simply by improving their test-taking skills. In plain English, *you can get better grades without studying more.*

Let me repeat that, because it's the essence of this book: **you can get better grades without studying more**. Learn it, believe it. This book will give you some tips to study more effectively, but more importantly, it will teach you *how* to write tests better. As a matter of fact, I believe you can get better grades and study *less* than you currently are. Really.

It's likely you know someone who never seems to study, but does well on an exam. Or, to add insult to injury, they borrow your notes the night before the exam and then beat you on the test? This is often chalked up to luck or IQ. "That guy's just naturally smart. He can get away without doing much work."

Don't believe it. The people who can do much with little often share surprising traits. They don't like to study. Or they're lazy. Or they have many other interests or obligations that prevent them from dedicating much time to studying. The difference between these people and the people who study a LOT and do poorly is this: *they have a system.*

> These "lucky" people who don't have to study are not smarter. They simply have systems for learning material, and writing exams. The difference between them and you is nothing more than a system.

This book is that system, and you can start putting the system to work for you in just a few hours. Don't be scared by the word "system" – this is neither complicated nor time-consuming. In fact, it's the opposite: easy and time *creating*. This is a simple method to prepare for and write multiple choice exams that anyone can master.

Why Multiple Choice?

Good question. There are many different types of tests and exams – essay, short answer and true/false, to name a few. What's so special about multiple choice?

- Multiple choice exams require a unique way of organizing, learning, and recalling your material.

- Multiple choice exams require you to approach your exam in a specific way for best results.

- Multiple choice questions require a specific, learnable type of thinking that is independent of the subject material and how well you know it.

In other words, your success at multiple choice exams depends not just on how well you know your material, **but how well you can write the test**.

What This Book Is

- A proven system for getting more from every bit of studying you do.

- A specific way of preparing for and writing multiple choice exams.
- A set of very focused techniques for dealing with the challenges unique to multiple choice style questions.
- A way of looking at how you learn and recall information that works best for multiple choice exams.

What This Book Isn't

- A "memory system"
- A vague "study tips" guide
- Difficult
- Time consuming

Who This Book Is For

- College and university students
- Adult learners
- High school students
- Professionals pursuing licensing
- Grad school applicants
- Anyone who suffers from test anxiety

Why Are Multiple Choice Tests So Common?

The invention of the multiple choice test format is attributed to Frederick J. Kelly at the University of Kansas in 1914. The great need at the time was to find an efficient way to assess the different talents of World War I military recruits. Multiple choice offered a quick way to test and score ability *en masse*, and was quickly adopted for other purposes, such as educational testing, which is likely what led you to this book. And while the First World War may be long over, multiple choice testing is increasing with each passing day.

Believe it or not, teachers and professors are just like us — they're short on time, under pressure, and more or less just want to lead a happy life.

Multiple choice tests offer these overworked academics an easier, faster way to get the numbers they need to create your grades. If you've got 2000 students in a course, using a computer to mark all the multiple choice tests in a few seconds is definitely easier than wading through pages of essay-type responses.

And, supposedly, they're *objective*. So your results shouldn't be affected by a tired TA, or an instructor who doesn't like you. And they shouldn't be affected whether your paper is marked by a 10 year old or a computer.

So they should be fair to everyone, right? No teacher's pet marks, no marks for eloquence.

Wrong. For many people, multiple choice tests are hard by virtue of their format. And that makes them anything but objective.

When you write a multiple choice exam, you're not just being tested on history, welding, truck driving, physics, or math. You're being tested on your ability to read (and how fast you can do it), and your ability to apply rules of logic to written statements. In addition to chemistry you're being tested on *how well you write tests*.

And if you don't write them well, you're at a disadvantage.

> **When you write a multiple choice exam, you're not just being tested on the subject matter. You're being tested on how well you write tests.**

Why Are Multiple Choice Tests Hard?

The fact is they can be very hard. Here are just a few reasons why multiple choice tests may be giving you grief:

- *Overconfidence* – you think multiple choice tests are easy, so you study less.
- *Trickery* – your professor thinks that multiple choice tests are easy, so they create tricky, confusing questions.
- *Time Pressures* – multiple choice tests are often intentionally lengthened. We've all felt this one.
- *Broader range* – the questions are short and fast, so a LOT of ground can be covered in one exam.
- *Specific data* – Since the answers are right there on the page (yup, it's true), specifics like dates, names and places become fair game.
- *Can't bluff* – No BS on these suckers. No part marks. No bonuses for writing an eloquent sentence to disguise the fact that you have absolutely no idea what the answer is.
- *Difficult for teacher to write* – That's right. Creating a good multiple choice test is a skill. And not all professors have it.
- *Content is shuffled* – many multiple choice tests have no structure whatsoever. You could be answering a physics question and a history question back to back. That's hard on the noggin.

Why Should They Be Easy?

Sound bleak so far? Here's the good news: from here on in, it's all about how to beat the multiple choice test format. To start our new optimistic outlook, here are a few reasons why the phrase "multiple choice" should be music to your ears:

- *The Answer Is Given To You* – That's right. Somewhere in the list of responses is the right answer. What could be easier?
- *You Can Guess* – You may hear that you shouldn't guess. I'm telling you right now it's not true. This book will teach you how to guess *properly*.
- *Basic Brainwork* – Many multiple choice exams tend to emphasize basic definitions or simple comparisons, rather than asking students to analyze new information or apply theories to new situations. In other words, they're often easier.
- *More Questions – What! I thought more questions made it harder!* That may be true, but more questions means each question is worth less overall. That lowers your risk on each question.
- *Grammar Don't Count* – You don't have to be Shakespeare to write multiple choice. At the most you just have to neatly color in circles. So you don't have to be Picasso either.

Success Factors

So you're telling me multiple choice tests are easy and hard?
Pretty much. Isn't this helpful so far?

It's true, though. So what this book will do is focus on using the easy stuff to your advantage, and making the hard stuff a little easier. Now, how well you do this depends on a number of factors. This book will help you with:

- *Prep* – Ugh. Studying. I'm not going to suggest you study more or less than you do now, because I don't know how much you're doing. Although I secretly believe you can do less. What you do need to do is study *smarter*.

- *Confidence* – Research shows that this is the key factor in...well, pretty much everything. Confidence is the single largest factor in effective memory!
- *Panic Management* – The better you control this, the more effective you'll be.
- *Time Management* – These tests can be long, and hard. Mismanaging your time can kill you on objective tests.
- *Practice* – Yup. Just like throwing a baseball and playing the oboe, multiple choice ability improves with practice.
- *Logic* – Multiple choice tests are all about logic. Understanding what something like "never not unnecessary" means can change your grade.
- *Test Strategies* – The meat of this book. The tips and techniques to help you through any multiple choice tests.

The Answers To YOUR Questions

If you're reading this book, I'll bet you're looking for answers. And I'll bet the questions to those answers look something like this:

- "I'm busy. I don't have time to study more. How can I get better grades without studying more than I already am?"

- "I'm so frustrated. I feel like I know the material, but every time I write a multiple choice exam I do worse than I should. I do fine on written exams, like essays. How can I do better at multiple choice?"

- "I just keep studying more and more, but my grades aren't improving. How can I find a way do better without burning out?"

- "There's a guy in my course who never seems to study. I don't even think he goes to class. I don't know whether I want to kill him, or be just like him. How does he do it?"

- "As soon as I start a multiple choice exam, I go blank. I read a few questions, and start to panic. How can I keep it together?"

- "I'm an adult. I've got a career, a family, and a mortgage. Plus it's been years since I was a student. I'm taking a course to advance my career, but the exams are killing me. How can I study quickly and effectively, and figure out how to deal with these crazy multiple choice exams?"

Any of these sound familiar? *Mastering Multiple Choice* will help with all of these, and many more. Let's get started.

GETTING STARTED

Anatomy Of A Question

Multiple choice tests have their own fancy jargon. The question itself is called the *stem*. The various options available to choose from are called *foils*. The correct foil is the *key*, and all the incorrect ones are called *distractors*. Finally, the whole package of stem and foils together is called an *item*. Here's an example:

Multiple choice tests can be:
   a) Easier than essay-type exams because they often emphasize general information
   b) Harder than essay-type exams because the time pressures are greater
   c) Easier or harder depending on the student and test developer
   d) All of the above

For our purposes, we'll avoid the term "foils" and use "options" instead.

How To Use This Guide

This book is built on three *Mastery Principles*. Each Mastery Principle is a piece of your overall strategy for complete exam success. Within each Mastery Principle are a series of core strategies. By learning and applying these core strategies, you'll become successful in each of the Mastery Principles.

The Mastery Principles are, in order:

   1. **Principle One: Master Your Material**
      This is the "before the exam" section. It deals with how to organize and learn your subject matter. Textbooks, notes, lectures – whatever makes up the content that

you'll be tested on. The objective here is to learn more quickly and effectively, in a way particularly suited to multiple choice exams.

2. **Principle Two: Master Test-Taking**
   How you "take the test" is critical. In this section, you'll learn how to write exams more quickly, recall more of what you studied, and ensure that you never run out of time on an exam again.

3. **Principle Three: Master The Questions**
   In this section you'll learn how to analyze the actual questions themselves, avoiding word traps, and finding the right answer *even when you haven't studied enough.*

What's the most important thing about this list? *It's in priority sequence.* In other words, the Mastery Principles at the top will have greater impact on your outcome than the ones on the bottom. So, if you have an exam tomorrow you can skip to the last section, but you'll be missing out on the best stuff.

Each of the Mastery Principles is like a position on a long lever. The farther out the lever you move, the more leverage you get, and the easier it is to do more work with the same effort. So you'll get more mileage out of Mastering Test-Taking, if you've already Mastered Your Material.

Remember: *most people fail exams before they get there.*

Most people fail exams before they get there.

You can dramatically improve your exam results simply by changing how you prepare, and how you take the test. Even if you don't change how you study, you'll notice a significant difference in your results simply by following the techniques in Principle II: Master Test-Taking. A small shift in your approach can generate enormous return.

Focus on Mastering Your Material and Mastering Test-Taking. These are the areas where you'll learn to work smarter not harder, and they'll determine your success in later areas. Then use the specific techniques in Mastering The Questions to crank up your grades even further.

Through all of this, remember that multiple choice test-taking is a *skill*. It improves with practice and knowledge.

Good luck!

Principle I:
Master Your Material

PRINCIPLE I: MASTER YOUR MATERIAL

U NFORTUNATELY, THIS BOOK ISN'T GOING to get you out of studying. All things considered, the better prepared you are for an exam, the better you'll do. However, if you focus on the techniques in this section, you can:

- Spend less time studying.
- Learn more in each hour you spend studying.
- Learn more the first time you see information – like during classes and lectures.
- Increase the speed at which you can review material.
- Understand material, instead of memorizing it.
- Increase your retention of material.
- Increase the speed and amount of recall at test time.

What <u>Mastering Your Material</u> is really about is this:
- Reducing the quantity of material you have to study.
- Increasing your understanding of it.
- Learning by using the multiple choice format.

In other words, rather than teach you to make a detailed study schedule to ensure you log so many hours on such and such a course, we'll focus on learning to condense and organize your material so you can learn more effectively, while at the same time getting your brain into multiple choice gear.

Forget about studying. Your new objective to <u>understand</u>.

Structuring

The biggest mistake most students make happens the *moment* that they start studying. The mistake they make is in the approach to the material.

If you're like most students, you've got a textbook or two (or three or seven) to learn for an exam, along with all the handouts from class, and the binder full of notes you took (if you showed up – if not, you'll have a binder full of photocopied notes from someone who took pity on you). That's a lot of material – likely hundreds of pages.

The common way to plow through this material is to read it. Then read it again. And when you wake up face down in a puddle of drool, start reading again.

Wrong. Most brains can remember only so much raw, unstructured material. The key to improving your exam scores lies in retention – what can you recall when the paper is in front of you and the clock is ticking?

The key to *retention* however, lies in *comprehension*. How well do you *understand* the material? And how well do you understand how well the various pieces of material relate to each other?

The ticket to increasing comprehension and retention while studying is in *structuring*.

What follows is a seven step method for reading, organizing, condensing and reviewing your study material that reduces what you need to cover, increases your understanding and retention, and helps practice the multiple choice format *all at the same time*.

The 7-Step Structuring System

The system we'll use for structuring is to use multiple passes through the material. Try this 7-step system for your course handouts and notes:

1. Read the table of contents or outline if there is one. Look at the headings, subheadings, etc. Is there a logical breakdown of the material?

2. Skim through *all* the pages. Take an hour if you need to. Look for headings, subheadings. Don't write. Just get a feel for how things are organized.

3. Skim through again with a couple of highlighters. Highlight all the headings you found. Use different colors for headings, sub headings, sub-sub headings, etc.

4. Go through again with a pen. Make a structured "table of contents" on a separate piece of paper. Just the headings and subheadings – no content. This is the structure of the course!

5. Start reviewing the content. Use a different highlighter to highlight important content in each section. That way you don't have to read everything again.

6. On your next pass, start writing **point form, essential content** into the table of contents that you created. This will become your core study document. Keep it concise.

7. **Use the core document for all studying.** Quiz yourself, and only refer to your original notes or textbook when you absolutely have to.

The 7-Step Structuring System: An Example

Here's an example. Which of the following is easier to understand, and faster to review while studying – A or B?

A.
Mastering Multiple Choice covers several mastery areas such as effective mastery of study materials, systems for approaching multiple choice exams, and ways of dealing with specific multiple choice questions. Each mastery area also includes a number of techniques. Mastering Your Material, for example, deals with such strategies as structuring, anti-study schedules, and visual thinking to name a few. Mastering Test-Taking focuses on cycling through exams, knowing when to guess, managing anxiety and several others. Finally, Mastering Questions looks at numerous specific strategies for dealing with questions and wording – modifiers, negatives, elimination, etc.

B.
Mastering Multiple Choice
- **Mastering Material**
  - Structuring
  - Anti-Study Schedules
  - Visual Thinking
- **Mastering Test-Taking**
  - Cycling
  - When to guess
  - Managing anxiety
- **Mastering Questions**
  - Modifiers
  - Negatives
  - Elimination

The second version (B), in structured form, contains almost identical content to the first version, but can be read, understood, reviewed and recalled much more quickly and easily.

Another benefit of the structuring technique is that it puts material in a format that's similar to the exam itself.   For example, let's structure the top level content of this book:

Mastery Principles:
- Mastering your material
- Mastering test-taking
- Mastering multiple choice questions

Does this structural breakdown of the material look familiar to you?   When you properly structure material, *it often tends to resemble a multiple choice exam.*   Throw in a quick "all of the above", and you've got a multiple choice question where every option is correct:

Which of the following is a Mastery Principle?
a) Mastering your material
b) Mastering test-taking
c) Mastering multiple choice questions
d) All of the above

This similarity will come in handy at exam time.   Dealing with material in the same point-form, abridged format when studying helps get your brain in the groove for the real thing.

7-Step Hints:

Did Someone Else Already Do the Work for You?
Many times, the structuring work is done for you already.   Don't forget to check the table of contents, course syllabus, or any other overviews.   You may find the structure laid out for you already!

Ditch Your Textbooks

One of the benefits of making great study notes is that you can carry a whole course around in your pocket, and review it all in just a few minutes.

If you're spending hours re-reading your textbooks, you're not studying effectively. Once you've compiled your core study document, you should only have to refer to the text for details you've forgotten, or for clarification.

Anti-Study Schedules

Here's an excellent system for getting the most out of study schedules: **never use them**.

Just about every study tip guide on the market will tell you to make a schedule for the week, and then allocate time blocks to certain subjects, or certain components of a given topic.

Baloney. Study schedules are garbage, and here's why:

- Study schedules weight the difficulty of everything the same.
- Study schedules assume your brain works with equal effectiveness at all times.
- Study schedules don't properly weight your existing knowledge of a topic.
- Study schedules create a false sense of productivity.
- Study schedules lower your morale when you can't stick to them (which most people can't).
- Study schedules don't allow for the real world.
- Study schedules lead to wasted time.

Do not use study schedules. They are a waste of your time.

The ultimate study schedule would be one which changed every second to take into account what you just learned and that that you now need slightly less time for that subject or topic. Since that's not practical, you'll need to self-monitor. Don't just read stuff for the sake of reading, and don't just make schedules because that's what everyone else does.

If you absolutely can't live without scheduling your life, then let's try to make your schedule more effective:

- Make the schedule tight, and aggressive.
- Don't schedule time for "general studying".
- Schedule time for building your structured master document.
- If you can't stay focused, switch to another topic, and start the master document for it. Not everyone can focus on the same material for hours at a time.
- Be aware. When you glaze over, get tired, or your attention wanders, it's VERY difficult to *force* yourself to focus. Take a break, or switch topics.

Don't study if you're not learning. Period. Staring at the page is not helping you.

Visual Thinking

There are mountains of research out there to suggest that we all learn and process information differently. While some people prefer text, others find pictorial representations easier to grasp.

One particularly useful structuring tool is to organize your main headings in a more graphical and less linear, format.

Remember our structuring example? Here's the same information presented in a more visual manner:

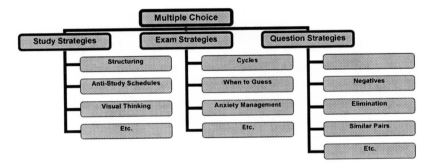

If this looks appealing to you, then you're likely a visual learner. If this just looks annoying, then stick to the previous outline format.

Focus On Understanding, Not Memorizing

Why is it that you can remember some things and not others? How is it that some things just seem to stick in your memory, while others seem to vanish as quickly as they arrive? There's no shortage of entire books on this subject, and the truth is, we still don't really know. What we *do* know is that it's a heck of a lot easier to remember things that you *understand*.

Learning by memorizing vast quantities of information is hard, unrewarding work. Most students find they can really only remember so much information for so long.

For example, what if I asked you to remember the following sequence?

- open
- sit
- insert
- turn
- move
- press
- turn

You probably can remember this for a while – your short-term memory will hang on to them, particularly if you repeat it out loud.

If I ask you tomorrow, though, or even 10 minutes from now, you likely won't remember at all.

But if you *understood* that this was the series of action you needed to perform to drive a car, you'd like have a much greater chance of recalling these actions:

- **Open** the car door
- **Sit** in the driver's seat
- **Insert** the key
- **Turn** the key

- **Move** the gearshift
- **Press** the gas pedal
- **Turn** the steering wheel

You might thing it's just memory trick — that you can visualize these actions, and therefore remember them more easily — but it works for other things. Try learning a physics or math formula from first principles. If you can do that, you'll know the formula anytime, and not have to rely on questionable short-term memory during an exam.

Try to remain consciously aware of your studying. When you find yourself skimming something without truly comprehending it, or trying to simply memorize without understanding, take a break or switch topics. Return later with a fresh focus to where you left off.

Study In The Same Mode

"For results that are best
study the same as the test."

Okay — not the best poetry, but there's truth there. Part of the key to multiple choice testing is to master the format. You need to get comfortable with the question types, the quirky wording, the "all of the aboves" and "none of the aboves".

The best way to reach that comfort level is to study using multiple choice tests themselves. (By the way, a side benefit of this is that questions are often recycled — you'll end up seeing some of the same questions that you studied from on your real exams.)

It's worth the time it takes to track down multiple choice exams for your area of study.

Sources of multiple choice tests:

- *Old exams*: Finding these tests is usually not hard. Old exams are almost always floating around through the student population.
- *Your Prof*: Ask them for old tests. Ask them for sample questions. Ask them for practice questions.
- *Text books*: They often contain sample tests
- *Online*: There are *thousands* of multiple choice tests online. They may not match your course content exactly, but they work.
- *Make your own*: Absolutely a great way to study. Get a group together, and have each person make questions on a section. Copy them, pass them out. The more people you have, the more questions you get.

Studying from other multiple choice tests is one of the best ways to ensure your success.

Practice For Real

Like most good students, you've probably managed to dig up a bunch of old or practice exams. Make the most of them! Take the tests for real. Give yourself the allotted amount of time, put away all your books and notes, and complete the exam as if it's the real deal. How much better practice can you get?

Mastering Your Material: 4 Critical Themes

Here are four themes that characterize excellent multiple choice preparation:

- *Use Successive Condensing*
  One of the critical factors of mastering you material is to continually have less of it on paper, and more of it in your head.   I call this *successive condensing*. Your study notes should continually shrink until they become a very simple outline.   Imagine that information is entering your brain, and leaving the page.

- *Limit Your Time*
  Your exam time is limited, why shouldn't your study time be, too?   This goes against conventional thinking, but why give yourself unlimited time? We all know that what we have to do has a tendency to expand to fit the time available.   If you give yourself all day to learn material for your statistics class, it's going to take all day.

  Wouldn't you rather learn it all in half the time, and spend some time doing other things?

- *Understand, Don't Memorize*
  Try to learn, not memorize.   Seek to understand the relationships between things.

- *Structure Your Material*
  Break the material into categories and headings. Try to take all of your course content, and fit it on one page in the form of a diagram, or a nested table of contents-style outline.

Mastering Your Material: 5 Common Pitfalls

Watch for these common mistakes when preparing for your next exam:

- Rigid study schedules.
- Reading and re-reading (writing too little).
- Writing too much (not condensing).
- Giving yourself too much time to study.
- Memorizing instead of understanding.
- Staring at the same pages over and over.

Principle II:
Master Test-Taking

PRINCIPLE II: MASTER TEST-TAKING

T HIS SET OF TIPS IS geared towards overall multiple choice "test-taking". Don't overlook these – they are arguably the most important of all the techniques in this book. Your biggest bang for your buck is contained here.

The Benefits Of Mastering Test-Taking:

- Finish every exam on time.
- Learn how and when to guess if necessary.
- Reduce or eliminate test anxiety.
- Increase your recall of course material.

Brain Dumps

So. You've crammed every last minute equation, name, date and rule into your short-term memory moments before entering the exam. What happens to that stuff? The simple answer is that it vanishes, and fast. Be forewarned: it will NOT last through the entire test. At least not all of it.

The easiest way to keep this stuff for the duration of your exam is to get it down on paper ASAP. And for this, your ideal tool is the brain dump.

As soon as permissible after you sit down at your desk in the exam, start writing. Use the scrap paper that's usually provided, or bring your own. If you have to, use the back of your exam booklet. What do you write? All that crucial data – formulas, equations, bits of last minute info that you just read.

Why bother? Getting it on paper serves two purposes. First, it locks it in before it drains from your memory or becomes clouded, and second, it clears your mind to focus on the task at hand: writing the exam.

Read The Directions

You've heard the adage, "Never assume anything." It applies to multiple choice tests as well. Even though your instructions are probably the same old yada yada about filling in the bubbles correctly, not all tests are created equal. Here are some instances to watch for:

Can more than one answer be correct? This does happen, and if you miss it, you'll be beating yourself to death trying to pick the *best* answer when there isn't one.

What are the time constraints? Many a student has stretched out their exam over a whole two hours only to discover that there is another part to be completed that they haven't even received yet.

Are there penalties for incorrect answers? If so, you need to adjust your strategy accordingly.

Answer ALL Questions, Unless...

Fill in all those bubbles. Circle something. Click on something. Whatever the answer format, even *guessing* is better than leaving a question blank.

The exception to this rule is when there are...

...Penalties For Incorrect Answers

You'll read and hear people say, "Don't guess. You're penalized for guessing."

DON'T BELIEVE IT. Many multiple choice tests do penalize for *incorrect* answers, but that doesn't mean you shouldn't answer a question if you're not sure. A little math will help make this a little clearer.

For instructors, one of the disadvantages of multiple choice exams is that you can guess. And if you guess, you might guess correctly. And that means your mark will be higher, even though you didn't know the precise answer.

For example, imagine a multiple choice test with only two options (a and b) for each stem. If you closed your eyes and guessed at every question, the laws of probability state you would actually get somewhere in the neighborhood of 50%. It would be like flipping a coin. If you do it enough times, the number of heads and tails will eventually be even. For a test with 3 options (a, b, c), random guessing would give you about 33.33 %. Four options (a,b,c,d) gives you 25%. And so on.

In order to combat this, test-makers will deduct marks for questions you get wrong. They claim this is to offset the "luck" factor. True, but what they don't tell you is that they just don't *want* you to guess. This "negative marking" makes many people scared to guess unless they are absolutely sure.

The good news is, there's a simple way to decide when to guess.

The decision of whether or not to guess is determined by comparing the odds of guessing correctly versus the amount deducted for an incorrect answer. If the odds of guessing correctly are equal to or greater than the amount deducted, you should guess!

The formula:

Amount deducted= x
# of options remaining after you eliminate = z

If $x < 1/z$, you should guess!

Before you email me complaining about math problems, here's the formula in plain English. **If the amount deducted for an incorrect answer is less than 1 divided by the number of options you've narrowed it down to, then start guessing.**

An example will help:

> **Q:** A multiple choice test penalizes you 1/3 of a mark for each incorrect answer. When should you guess?
> **A:** Anytime you can narrow down to 3 options or less (1/z, or 1/3).

The toughest tests will penalize you a full mark for an incorrect answer. In those cases, you pretty much need to know the answer. Or feel really lucky.

Make sure you know when to guess *before you start writing*. Do the math right at the beginning of the exam, or better still, ask ahead of time what the marking structure will be.

Time Management

In order to compensate for what they feel is an "easy" type of test, some instructors will place extreme time pressures on exams by having huge numbers of questions in a given time period.

The "Cycle" strategy, below, works wonders to beat this. However, you still need to use some basic time management principles to make sure you don't get caught short.

- *How much is available?* Make sure you know. Read the instructions, and ask if you're still not sure.
- *Bring a Watch.* Sounds simple, but you never know whether you'll be able to see a clock or not, and *wondering* what time it is will kill your concentration.
- *How is the test structured?* Are there different sections? Do they differ in their question type, or difficulty, or their "worth". If some questions are worth twice as much, make sure you allocate sufficient time, as these questions are likely more time consuming.
- *Leave some time for checking your work.* Even just a few minutes to ensure that you answered all the questions can gain you a few marks.

Should I Stay or Should I Go? Most traditional exam advice says to stay and double/triple-check your work until the bitter end. While this doesn't hurt with written format exams, you don't get nearly as much return on multiple choice tests by staring at all the little dots. Use your instincts. If you've got two more exams this afternoon and four more next week, you may be better off taking a break or using the time to study.

(Besides, there's a certain level of confidence and satisfaction from getting up early and walking out while everyone else is still panicking and second-guessing!)

Cycle Through The Test

How you "take" the test can affect your marks more than any other factor. The cycle method works like this: instead of completing the test in numerical order, or in a "linear" fashion, you work through the entire test numerous times. It's as simple as can be, but many people resist this approach. Don't resist. Allow yourself to be flexible. Give it a try on some practice exams.

The "cycle" approach to multiple choice testing is extremely beneficial for a number of reasons:

- It makes maximum use of your time.
- It boosts confidence, and reduces test anxiety.
- It helps with information recall.
- It ensures you won't get "caught short" by the clock.
- Information found later in the test questions can help you with earlier problems.

The cycle system:
  1. **Scan** – this is the quickest cycle through the test, during which you do NOT answer any questions. Take one to three minutes to skim the test, observing the structure, the question styles, the number of options, and the overall length. Don't read the questions. Just skim for structure and length. Do NOT omit this pass – it's here that you'll create the entire foundation of your approach to the exam.

2. **Easy** – This can be the most encouraging or most terrifying pass of the exam, but it's crucial. The idea during this second pass is to answer all the questions that you know the answer to almost immediately. In other words, don't spend any longer than the moment it takes to read the question and options. Don't be concerned if it feels like you're only answering a handful of questions – there's a good reason for this technique.

   Hint: mark all the unanswered questions with a "?" in pencil so you don't have to waste valuable time on your next passes through comparing the answer key with the question page.

3. **Harder** – Once you've completed the "easy" pass, return to the start of the test. Start working your way through the remaining question. You'll be surprised at how many answers seem more obvious on this pass.

   As with the Easy pass, don't be afraid to skip any questions that you just can't pin down. Remember that the Cycle system creates plenty of time to come back to them. The key is to focus on the marks you can get first, and save the rest for later.

   Hint: erase the "?" from the questions you answer!

4. **Final** – The final phase is where two things happen. First, you build on the momentum, knowledge and mindset of the previous steps, and answer any final questions. The other thing that happens during this stage is that you guess. That's right – when all else fails, guess. How to guess *wisely* is something you'll learn in the techniques section of this book.

Modifying The Cycle System

Don't be afraid to add more cycles. You might pass through the test a dozen times, answering a few questions each time, letting your brain work, and looking for answers elsewhere in the test. Just don't add *fewer* cycles — you'll end up back in the same old rut of running out of time.

> **If you only implement one strategy in this book, make it this one. The Cycle System can dramatically improve your results.**

Test Anxiety And The Cycle System

The Cycle System is perhaps the most important strategy in this book. A note of caution, however, for those who are prone to test anxiety:

You must trust the system.

The first two cycles through the exam are often very quick. You're not meant to answer questions on the first pass, but even on the second pass many students don't answer too many questions.

This is where panic often sets in — don't allow it to fluster you. Each successive pass will reveal more information to you. With each cycle you'll find yourself remembering more, and answering more. Trust the system, and remember, this is an effective way to use your time.

If you've never used this approach, give it an honest try before you dismiss it. Get a practice test and try the cycle system out. Time yourself, and follow the procedure until you're done the exam.

Test Anxiety

We've all felt moments of panic in our lives. Remember the symptoms? Dry mouth, sweaty palms, weak knees, blank mind....hang on! *Blank mind?*

It's true. Nothing will drain all that hard earned knowledge from your mind like a little panic, thanks to a handy little apparatus in our brain called the amygdala. It's that sucker that's responsible for the "fight or flight" response to stress. And although it's deadly during exams, don't knock it – it's what allowed your ancestors to survive long enough to procreate, and have offspring like you.

When faced with danger (stress), the amygdala takes over, rerouting the vital resources of the body to either *fight* or *flight*. And regardless of which choice is made, the result is generally the same: the supply chain to the brain is cut back so the muscles can fulfill their crucial role of keeping you alive.

So, when you panic during an exam, your brain gets shut down. Simple as that.

If you're using the Cycle method to do your exam, you're already a long way toward reducing test anxiety, but here are a few others:

Expect the Unexpected

The techniques in this guide will help manage what they call "test anxiety", but the best trick I've found is to *expect to be flustered.*

Remember that the exam in front of you was designed by someone else. You *can't* anticipate all the questions. On top of this, many exams are designed not just to test your knowledge, but to deceive you. To push your limits.

So forget about it. Go with the flow. Expect that there will be *many* questions you can't answer on your first pass. Expect that there may be material you swear was never in any book or lecture. Just use the multi-pass system, and the techniques, and work your way through.

Hit Your Stride

If you can't forget about it – and really, who can? – then believe this: your ability to answer multiple choice questions improves dramatically over the course of the exam. If you've ever participated in any kind of physical endurance sport, like distance running, you'll notice that it takes a while to hit your stride. Distance runners often feel better several miles into the race then they do at the start, and the same principle applies to multiple choice exams. If you start to do questions and you feel a sense of panic, just keep at it. Skip the ones you can't answer, and go back to them later.

Multiple choice exams often require a certain set of logic processes. Your brain has to compare, contrast, eliminate and assess true false characteristics. It has to process if/then scenarios, and deal with those icky "none of the above/all of the above" logic games. The first few questions sometimes seem tough because you haven't hit your stride, but the more your brain uses these processes, the easier they become to apply to successive questions.

Use the multi-pass system with the belief that your brain will shift more and more into a mode that allows you to answer the questions, and retrieve the information you studied.

Write Your Own Exam

Picture this. You're two hours into a three hour exam. You're pressed for time – it's a long test, challenging in length and content. You know it's going to be tight.

And the guy beside you stands up, hands in his papers, and leaves. Just like that.

How can he be done? Ohmigod I'm a failure. Gaaaccck! I'm never going to...

Sound familiar? The key to learning how to compete with your peers is to not compete. Forget about it. Just like you run your own race, you need to write your own test. For all you know, the genius-speed-reader-scholarship-pro who left at the two hour mark is outside crying because he only answered a third of the questions.

Stay focused on your own work. Stay as long as you need to. Do what you need to do to work the test in your favor.

Positive Attitude

No matter what happens believe that you can and will do well on the exam. Write it on your hand if you have to, but believe it.

Ask Questions

Don't be afraid to stick your arm up and ask questions. Instructors and exams are not perfect, so if you don't understand something, ask. It may make the difference of a few marks. (And chances are, there are a bunch of shy, confused people who'll thank you for asking the question.) Don't get carried away with this one – multiple choice tests are notorious for being vague, and part of not reading too much into them is not asking too many questions.

But when you do have a question, remember, professors are also notorious for giving away crucial details when asked.

Principle III:
Master The Questions

PRINCIPLE III: MASTER THE QUESTIONS

T HIS SECTION FOCUSES ON ITEM-specific techniques. In other words, it looks at the nitty-gritty strategies for dealing with the actual questions on the exam. As with the Master Test-Taking section, some of these techniques may seem awkward for you, and that's fine – you may not want to adopt them all. Before you discount a strategy, however, give it a try on a practice exam.

Disclaimer: A good test designer knows these tricks as well as you do. Although these techniques may dramatically help some students, the best "return" on your time is to closely follow the Master Your Material, and Master Test-Taking sections. They are powerful tools that will work regardless of the skill of the test designer.

The Process Of Elimination

The standard mindset for any kind of testing is to come up with the right answer. Right? Well, that's certainly a valid approach. After all, if you come up with all the right answers, then you'll get a perfect score. What could be easier?

Welcome to reality. In the real world, people don't know all the right answers. You may not even know *most* of the right answers. However, we do know that in multiple choice exams, the answer is there *somewhere*. You just have to find it.

Finding the right answer can be like trying to remember something that's on the tip of your tongue. The more you think about it the more elusive it can be. Sometimes, to remember things, you need to come at them...well, sort of sideways.

The equivalent process in multiple choice exams is called *Process of Elimination*, or POE. Using POE is simple. Instead of trying to find the right answer, simply try to find and eliminate the *wrong* ones. What's left must be correct.

Keep POE in mind as you work through the tips that follow. Remember you don't have to know the right answer to get a question right! If you can eliminate enough wrong options, you can find the right one, or at least put yourself in a better position to make an educated guess.

> **Multiple choice exams are as much about eliminating *wrong* answers as they are about finding *right* ones.**

What follows is a series of strategies for improving your ability to choose correct answers, and eliminate wrong ones.

Cover All Options When Reading

Good exam writing is all about focus. Try using a blank sheet of paper to cover up all the response options for the question. Just read the stem. This allows you to

- Focus solely on the wording of the question.
- Not be distracted or misled by some of the possible answers (remember, test-makers can be out to trick you).
- Use the next strategy...

...Read The Stem, Guess The Answer

Before you lift that paper to reveal your options, try to guess the correct answer. Anticipating the answer to the question may:

- Help you to recall the real answer from memory before the alternatives start to look confusingly similar.
- Keep you in an *active* mental mode. Remember, you're taking this test. It's not taking you.

Note: Some research suggests that one in three students will score better by using this strategy alone. One in three! Also, if you tend to do better on essay-style exams, this strategy may be very helpful for you.

Don't Answer Too Soon/ Read ALL the Responses

Once you've decided to reveal the possible answers, don't jump at the first correct one you see. There may be a "more correct" answer a little further down the list, or an "all of the above".

Always at least *consider* all the options.

Choose The BEST Answer

And while you're considering all the options, remember this general rule for multiple choice exams: you're looking for the *best* answer.

There will be questions where it seems as if all of the options are right. That's when you need to remember you're not looking for the *only* right answer. Just the best one. The one that's the "most right".

Draw From Course Content

Remember you're being tested on what you were taught, not on personal knowledge. Inevitably you're going to come across a time when the right answer on the exam really isn't...well it really isn't the right answer.

This can happen when you've got more knowledge in a subject area than the test designer, or when you've studied from resources outside of your course texts and notes. Not every expert has the same opinion, so you may find different facts, claims and theories in different sources.

Try to stick to course content. In *most* cases, that's where your exam questions are being derived from.

Get Your Pencil On The Paper

One of the biggest complaints from students about multiple choice exams is that they get confused by the wording and/or the options.

The easiest way to deal with this is to use a pencil to mark up your exam. Many of the techniques that follow work best when you get your pencil on the paper.

Don't be shy! For the length of the exam, that paper is yours. Mark it up. Cross things out, circle important words, make notes. If there are strict instructions to not mark the test paper, do it anyway. Write in pencil, and bring an eraser to erase your marks before handing it in. (This only takes a minute.)

Treat Every Option As A True / False

Another way to look at multiple choice exams is a series of True/False statements arranged in groups. If T/F questions are your style, you might find it beneficial to approach an exam in this way.

To do this, read the stem, and the first option as a single statement. For an example, we'll use the question shown earlier on:

Multiple choice tests can be
   a) Easier than essay-type exams because they often emphasize general information
   b) Harder than essay-type exams because the time pressures are greater
   c) Easier or harder depending on the student and test developer
   d) All of the above

To tackle this question using the T/F technique, take the stem and first response together:

"Multiple choice tests can be…easier that essay-type exams because they often emphasize general information."

True or False? True. Put a big letter "T" beside option (a), and proceed on to (b). Do the same.

In this case, the answers are all true, so the correct response is (d).

Circle Key Words

The wording in multiple choice exams can be crucial. Words like "none" or "all" or "never" can change the whole sense of a statement (more on these later). Many a mark has been lost by missing one tiny word. Learning to recognize these words can make the difference.

Circle any words you think might be important, such as:

- Dates, places, names
- Superlatives like "best", "most"
- Qualifiers like "usually" or "often"
- Negatives and double negatives like "not unnecessary"
- Prefixes like "hyper-" or "dis-"

You'll find a longer list of key words in the tips to follow. For now, remember that actually using a pencil to emphasize these words can help you avoid misunderstanding a question.

Don't Linger / Do What You Know

Remember the "Cycling" approach to the exam. If you work the question and you don't know the answer immediately, move on. You'll get it on the second or third pass after your brain has had a chance to get in gear and process the question a little further.

Let Your Brain Warm Up

It's surprising how "cold" your brain is when you start an exam. Even though you may have been cramming for hours right up to the start of the exam, your brain really needs a bit of time to work itself into the "zone". Like any muscle in your body, your brain can benefit from a bit of warming up. For peak performance, professional athletes warm up their muscles before a competition – why wouldn't you, the professional "test-taker", warm up your brain?

By doing the easy questions first, you're giving yourself a chance to gear up for the hard ones.

Grammatical Errors

Some of the most common errors made by test designers are grammatical ones. Why? Well, most professors design their tests by coming up with a question and the correct response. Then they write three or four incorrect distractors as options. A good instructor will carefully read their stem with each option to make sure the grammar works with each of the distractors. A less conscientious test-maker won't.

While less common than they used to be, these are certainly worth keeping an eye out for. To take advantage of this, compare the stem and the possible responses, and look for errors in number, gender, etc.

Here are two types that may prove to be revealing on an exam:

Article inconsistency
The use of "a" versus "an" – if the stem ends in "an", then the correct answer is most likely to begin with a vowel.

E.g. *Multiple choice exams are* a...e*xcellent way to test student knowledge.*

Number inconsistency
Verbs in the stem such as "are" point to a plural response. A verb like "is" suggests a singular response.

E.g. *Multiple choice exam*s...is *more time consuming to grade.*

Rephrase In Your Own Words

Don't be afraid to rewrite what you see on the test. There are a million and one ways to write a sentence. Some are simple and straightforward. Others are complicated and confusing, and you can be sure your friend the test-maker will not always choose the easy way.

Read the sentence. Circle the key words. Ask yourself, "What is this sentence saying?" Then rewrite it, on the test paper if possible, in your own terms.

Look For Negatives

There's nothing less worse than not answering a question incorrectly.

Does that make sense to you? At first glance, this sentence is basically gibberish. But it does have a meaning.

On an exam, you may have to decipher statements like the one above just to understand the question before you even *start* trying to find the correct response. Single, double, even triple negatives are often used to complicate the meaning of the question. And misreading just one negative means the whole meaning of the statement is reversed!

The key to negatives is to rewrite the question. Let's look at the above phrase again, and identify the negatives:

There's <u>nothing</u> <u>less worse</u> than <u>not</u> answering a question <u>in</u>correctly.

Let's start with *less worse*. What does less worse mean? If something is less worse, it must be "better".

So *less worse=better*

What about *not* and the prefix *in*? The great thing about multiple negatives is that they cancel each other out. We can get rid of one negative from a sentence as long as we get rid of another one to keep the balance. As long as we do this in pairs, the meaning of the sentence stays the same.

So, stroke out *not* and *in*.

What does our sentence say now?

There's nothing better than answering a question correctly.

Simple, and easy to understand!

Here are some negative prefixes to keep an eye out for. In each case, the negative prefix changes the meaning of the word to its opposite.

Negative prefixes

Im-	Impossible means not possible.
Ir-	Irresponsible means not responsible.
Un-	Unnecessary means not necessary.
Dis-	Disabled means not able.
Non-	Nonalcoholic means not alcoholic.
In-	Inappropriate means not appropriate
Il-	Illegal means not legal.

Now if we come back to our question of multiple negatives, what happens when we combine a negative prefix word, with another negative, like "not"? Let's have a look:

Double Negatives

Not unnecesary	necessary
Not nonalcoholic	alcoholic
Not inappropriate	appropriate
Not impossible	possible

Not illegal	legal
Not irresponsible	responsible
Not disabled	able

The principle here, as mentioned above, is that double negatives cancel each other out.

Modifiers

Modifiers are certain words in the stem or response of a question that change the meaning. A solid understanding of modifiers is crucial to multiple choice success. Modifiers can include *limiters, superlatives* and *qualifiers.*

Limiters

A trick test designers will use is to make *most* of a response true to lure you into selecting it. This most commonly takes the form of a tiny detail – a *limiter* – that makes the statement false.

Common limiters include:
- dates
- names
- places

You'll find limiters in the stem, too, so watch for them. If a statement such as "The discovery of the new world by Columbus in 1482 was important because…" makes you rack the American history file in the dusty recesses of your brain, then look again.

Right away you can look for "none of the above", because the discovery was in 1492, not 82. There may be a list of compelling reasons why the discovery of the new world was important, but they are all automatically incorrect because of the limiter in the stem.

Superlatives/ Extreme Modifiers

Superlatives are words such as *every, all, none, always,* and *only.* They tend to make an answer false because it's harder to make a true statement using superlatives.

For example, "Bed rest and plenty of fluids is *always* the *best* treatment for a cold," is a statement that uses superlatives. Can you *really* be sure that bed rest and fluids is *always* the *best?* Might there be some situation where this isn't true?

A superlative in phrase makes it more difficult for a statement to be true.

Some superlatives to note:
- all
- none
- never
- best
- without exception
- absolutely
- always
- only
- nobody
- everybody
- worst
- certainly
- invariably
- absolutely not
- no one
- everyone
- certainly not

Qualifiers

At the other end of the scale from superlatives are *qualifiers.* They are less extreme than superlatives, and as such, tend to be more often correct.   They're words that *could* indicate a true state.

Let's look at our superlatives example, but replace the superlatives with qualifiers:

"Bed rest and plenty of fluids is *frequently* an effective treatment for a cold,"

The qualifier *frequently* makes the statement more "wishy-washy" than when it used the superlative.   It's harder to dispute a statement using qualifiers, and so they tend to be true.

Some qualifiers to note:
- usually
- frequently
- some
- possibly
- seldom
- many
- much
- often
- sometimes
- most
- might
- unlikely
- probably
- a majority
- likely to
- apt to
- a few
- may

If you're designing a test, it's easier to write a true statement using qualifiers than it is superlatives. Superlatives require a test-maker to be absolutely sure of their facts, so the lazy test-maker will fall back on qualifiers for cover. As a result, statements containing qualifiers may tend to be true more often.

"All Of The Aboves"

There are two ways to approach "All of the Aboves": negative and positive. They're both straightforward.

Negative
Simply look for a wrong answer. If you find even one response that doesn't work, you know then that *all of the above* is no longer a possibility.

Positive
Find two correct answers. This is a little more difficult (roughly twice as hard since you have to find two instead of one!) than the negative approach. If you find two correct answers, and there are no other qualifying responses (like "a and b but not c", etc.), then the correct answer must be *all of the above*.

"None Of The Aboves"

Using similar logic to "all of the aboves", simply find one *correct* answer, and you can assume that *none of the above* is NOT an option.

These tend to be more difficult. If you're not *positive* an answer is correct, it means you have to prove all the other responses false in order to select *none of the above*. Proving responses false is often challenging. Remember to look for superlatives – words like *always* and *never* tend to make a statement false. Qualifiers like *can* and *often* tend to make a statement true.

Multiple Correct Answers

Many students struggle with these. Examples of multiple correct answers are when you're given options that include something like "(a) & (c) are correct" or "(b) & (d), but not (e)".

There is normally no trick to these ones – they just require some concentration. If you have trouble with them, it's usually a matter of deciphering the responses, and keeping your head on straight while you figure out what fits.

This is another important time to get the pencil on the paper.
- Start by marking the given statements true or false.
- Go through the options, and cross out any that don't contain the first true statement (e.g. "b") as an option.
- Pick the next true statement letter (e.g. "e").
- Of the remaining response options, cross out any that don't contain "e".
- Repeat until you narrow down to one possible response.

Questions That State A Reason

Words in the question such as *since, because, when* or *if* tend to make a statement false. They state a reason, or justify a statement.

Pay close attention – the reason that is given may be incorrect or incomplete.

Tips For Math Questions

For many students, mathematical questions are a death toll. The questions are frequently word problems, and many students have difficulty finishing in time. Second-guessing your response seems to be a default condition of math questions.

Here are a few math-specific strategies:

Don't Do The Math

This secret to solving math questions on multiple choice exams may come as a surprise: *don't do the math unless you have to.*

Really. There are many "shortcut" techniques for dealing with numerical problems that can help circumnavigate a potentially time consuming math solution. These math shortcuts are actually quite helpful beyond the realm of multiple choice testing.

Try http://mathforum.org/ for tips and techniques. Remember all the other multiple choice strategies still apply. Use the process of elimination!

Trial And Error

Like all multiple choice questions, the beauty of math questions is that the answer is right there on the page. The added bonus with algebra-style math questions is that **the formula to find the answer is given to you**! Simply work your way through the formula systematically using each of the given answers until you find one that works.

$$\text{If } x^2+2x^3=63, \text{ then } x=$$

a) 2
b) 3
c) 4
d) 6

If you try the formula with each of the answers, you'll find that only 3 (answer 'b') gives the correct answer.

Similar Pairs Are A Clue

Let's take another look at how tests are usually developed.

First, the question is written, along with its correct response. The next line of thinking for most instructors is, "Okay, now I need to disguise this answer so it's not obvious."

The standard way to do this is to write responses that are as appealing as the correct one – responses that make sense, but are incorrect. And the most appealing incorrect response is one that is *almost* the same as the correct one, but not quite.

These similar pairs of responses can provide a clue that perhaps one of the two is correct.

"Funny" Responses Are Usually Wrong

This generally goes without saying. Humorous responses are usually there as "gifts" from the test-maker to narrow your number of choices or to provide a little stress relief and levity.

They're frequently wrong.

Numbered Responses

In questions that require a numerical response, the numbers at the extreme ends of the answers can often be ruled out by quick reckoning. Look for similar pairs and numbers in the middle range to be more frequently correct.

Long Passages

Particularly common in tests like the LSAT are long paragraphs followed by several questions that test your comprehension and retention of the paragraph. These types of questions can be especially challenging for students whose reading speed is slower, or who struggle with comprehension and retention.

A simple technique to use in these circumstances is to **skip the long paragraph(s) and read the questions first.** This allows you to find out what information is most relevant – essentially, it tells you what to look for when you're going through the passages.

Long passage questions are often found on examinations that push students with tight time restrictions. Any edge that allows you to skim faster through the long written portions can leave you extra time for other sections.

Odd One Out

Since there is only one correct answer to most questions, that answer has to be different from the other answers. So if you see two or three answers that all mean the same thing, they could be the wrong answers. (Careful: this trick doesn't always work!)

Don't Look For Patterns

First of all, they're likely not there. It's rare to discover a test with a response pattern (c,a,b,d...c,a,b,d...c,a,b,d, etc.). Any test designer that makes this mistake is likely to make many other mistakes, and the exam just won't be that hard.

Second, finding patterns means you need to know the correct answers! You might feel you've discovered a pattern, only to find later that it was based on some of your own incorrect answers.

Finally, searching for patterns takes too much time. By the time you discover that there is no pattern, you've burned up a lot of valuable time.

Longer Responses

It's often said that it takes longer to tell the truth. Some guides will tell you that the longer answer is more often correct. While this can be the case, it's not a foolproof strategy.

If All Else Fails, Pick C

Many instructors subconsciously feel that the correct answer is "hidden" better if it is surrounded by distractors, therefore response (a) or (d) is usually least likely to be the correct one.

Is this one true? There is actually some research to support that there is a slightly higher statistical incidence of (b) and (c) as correct responses. The key here, however, is that it's *very slight*, and probably not worth gambling on.

Your First Guess?

You've likely heard the adage, "Don't change your answer. Your first guess is usually right."

This advice is based on the notion that your brain knows the true answer before your consciousness, and once you start thinking about a problem, you may be led astray from the true answer.

While this may be true, research also shows that if you have a good reason to change your answer, then change it. Your first guess is only as good as the logic and facts you have to back it up.

COMMON PROBLEMS

COMMON PROBLEMS

O NE OF THE MOST ISOLATING and demoralizing experiences in education is to sit in an exam hall and slowly, painfully fail a test over the course of an hour or more, all the while feeling that *you are alone.*

Rest assured, you are not.

The anxiety you might feel staring at a multiple choice answer sheet is being felt across the room, throughout the school, and around the world. If you find multiple choice tests hard, it's because they *are*, and there's nothing wrong with you.

Let's take a look at the root causes and solutions to a number of common multiple choice exam challenges.

"I never get finished."

This is a Principle II problem – Mastering Test-Taking. Make sure you stick to the Cycle system of taking multiple passes through the material – don't waste too much time on questions that you can't answer in short order.

In addition to all the other benefits outlined in that section, the multi-pass technique does wonders for time management. It allows you to be constantly aware of how much you have to do in the time remaining. Stick to it and you'll finish on time every time.

"The questions were all on trivial details."

What's the essence of this one? Is the problem really that the questions were on trivial details, or that you didn't *know* the trivial details when the time came?

This is a Principle I problem – Mastering Your Material. There are several ways to deal with this:

- Get old tests, preferably by the same test-maker. Note the level of detail.
- Study in groups, in a trivia or "Jeopardy-style" format. This tends to bring the focus from large concepts down to the detail level.

"I can't read fast enough."

Let's dig into this one a bit. There's really no question that reading faster is an advantage in most things. But do you need to be a speed reader to succeed?

But let's just make sure you understand where the speed-reading advantage lies. (And to clarify, when I say speed reading, I'm assuming your retention and comprehension are also heightened

– in other words, if you're reading ninety miles an hour, but you can't remember or understand a word, then you're not speed reading. You're skimming, and likely not doing it well.)

Assuming that you legitimately increase your reading speed, then where this really makes a difference is in *writing* the test, not studying for it. As you know from learning how to Master Your Material, our goal is to reduce the amount of material you have to read, not re-read it at a faster rate. Your speed reading will pay off the first time you're reading your textbook or notes, but if you're using the principle of successive condensing, you should have less and less to read each time.

"All the answers seem right to me."

It's no surprise that this is a very common challenge. Test-makers generally want all the responses to look equally appealing to make it difficult to guess.

Here are your best strategies for dealing with this scenario:

1. *Practice the format* – Students who have a high degree of skill in multiple choice problems report that correct and incorrect responses have a "feel". With enough practice, you can learn to recognize the subtle differences in wording between the two formats.
2. *Cover the answers* – Read the question first, and try to come up with your own answer to the problem before looking at the options.
3. *Cycle through the exam* – Cycling helps reduce anxiety, and can provide the small bits of critical information that you need to distinguish between very similar responses.

Other Problems?

If you've got a problem not covered here, let me know. Submit your question to problems@masteringmultiplechoice.com or visit www.masteringmultiplechoice.com for more help.

SAMPLE TESTS AND QUESTIONS

I keep a growing list of links to free sample tests and questions at:

http://www.masteringmultiplechoice.com/multiple-choice-questions.html

It covers SAT, GMAT, LSAT, MCAT, GRED, TOEFL, ACT, and more. To try out your new skills, head on over there, pick your topic and get started!

CONCLUSION

THERE MAY BE A PART of you that thinks this is all deceitful, somehow. That using a "system" to do better on your exams feels a little bit like cheating. Don't believe that part of you.

The whole reason multiple choice exams exist is to serve the system. They provide a fast, inexpensive way to generate data (your marks) for an education system that lives and dies by the numbers. The system creates the tests and the rules. Your job is to do the best you can within those boundaries.

Interestingly, although multiple choice tests are often called "objective tests", the only part of them that is objective is the actual marking. Creating the exams and writing them – the important parts – are about as subjective and prone to errors and bias as you can get. Don't let a test-maker's mood, attitude, or lack of test-making skill affect your grades and your future.

The skills in the first part of this book, Mastering Your Material, touch on a much broader world than that of multiple choice exams. The ability to absorb, process, and communicate large quantities of information is the cornerstone of learning, and in this accelerated world, one thing is certain:

The future belongs to the learners.

Good luck,

Stephen Merritt
www.masteringmultiplechoice.com

CPSIA information can be obtained at www.ICGtesting.com
Printed in the USA
BVOW04s0125221114

376135BV00003B/924/P

9 780973 978216